W9-BSQ-163

RACIAL JUSTICE IN AMERICA

What Is ANTI-RACISM?

HEDREICH NICHOLS WITH KELISA WING

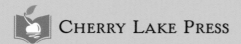

Published in the United States of America by Cherry Lake Publishing Group
Ann Arbor, Michigan
www.cherrylakepublishing.com

Reading Adviser: Marla Conn, MS, Ed., Literacy specialist, Read-Ability, Inc.
Content Adviser: Kelisa Wing
Book Design and Cover Art: Felicia Macheske

Photo Credits: © Daisy Daisy/Shutterstock.com, 5; © GagliardiPhotography/Shutterstock.com, 7; © Tina Gutierrez/
Shutterstock.com, 9; Library of Congress/Photograph by Edward S. Curtis, LOC Control No.:94504691, 13; Library of
Congress/Photograph by William R. Howell, LOC Control No.: 2016652289, 15; Library of Congress/Photograph by Arthur
Rothstein, LOC Control No.: 2017777149, 16; © Xackery Irving/Shutterstock.com, 19; © Motortion Films/Shutterstock.com,
21; © ryanbphotography/Shutterstock.com, 23; © Ira Bostic/Shutterstock.com, 25; © JeremySchwartz/Shutterstock.com, 31

Graphics Throughout: © debra hughes/Shutterstock.com; © GoodStudio/Shutterstock.com; © Natewimon Nantiwat/
Shutterstock.com; © Galyna_P/Shutterstock.com

Library of Congress Cataloging-in-Publication Data

Names: Nichols, Hendreich, author. | Wing, Kelisa, author.
Title: What is anti-racism? / Hendreich Nichols, Kelisa Wing.
Description: Ann Arbor, Michigan : Cherry Lake Publishing, 2021.
  | Series: Racial justice in America | Includes index. | Audience: Grades 4-6 |
  Summary: "Race in America has been avoided in children's education for too long. What Is Anti-Racism? explores the idea
  of actively working against racism in a comprehensive, honest, and age-appropriate way. Developed in conjunction with
  educator, advocate, and author Kelisa Wing to reach children of all races and encourage them to approach race issues
  with open eyes and minds. Includes 21st Century Skills and content, as well as a PBL activity across the Racial Justice in
  America series. Also includes a table of contents, glossary, index, author biography, sidebars, educational matter, and
  activities"— Provided by publisher.
Identifiers: LCCN 2020039993 (print) | LCCN 2020039994 (ebook) | ISBN 9781534180215 (hardcover) | ISBN 9781534181922
  (paperback) | ISBN 9781534181229 (pdf) | ISBN 9781534182936 (ebook)
Subjects: LCSH: Anti-racism—United States—Juvenile literature. | United
  States—Race relations—Juvenile literature.
Classification: LCC E184.A1 N494 2021 (print) | LCC E184.A1 (ebook) | DDC
  305.800973—dc23
LC record available at https://lccn.loc.gov/2020039993
LC ebook record available at https://lccn.loc.gov/2020039994

Cherry Lake Publishing Group would like to acknowledge the work of the Partnership for 21st Century Learning,
a Network of Battelle for Kids. Please visit http://www.battelleforkids.org/networks/p21 for more information.

Printed in the United States of America
Corporate Graphics

Many thanks to Tonja, Mervil, Kellie, and Traci.

Hedreich Nichols, author, educator, and host of the YouTube series on equity #SmallBites, is a retired
Grammy-nominated singer-songwriter turned EdTech teacher who uses her experience as a "one Black
friend" to help others understand race, equity, and how to celebrate diversity. When not educating and
advocating, she enjoys making music with her son, multi-instrumentalist @SwissChrisOnBass.

Kelisa Wing honorably served in the U.S. Army and has been an educator for 14 years. She is the author
of *Promises and Possibilities: Dismantling the School to Prison Pipeline*, *If I Could: Lessons for Navigating
an Unjust World*, and *Weeds & Seeds: How to Stay Positive in the Midst of Life's Storms*. She speaks both
nationally and internationally about discipline reform, equity, and student engagement. Kelisa lives in
Northern Virginia with her husband and two children.

CHAPTER 1

Anti-Racism: The Basics

Being treated badly because of the way you look isn't fair. And bullying someone because of their skin color or how they identify is wrong. That's what racism is— treating someone badly because of their skin color, culture, or identity. Mostly, no one wants to be racist. But what does being anti-racist mean? Isn't that the same as *not* being racist? If not being racist isn't enough, what else is there?

These are the kinds of questions you might think of when you hear the word *anti-racism* for the first time. The good thing is, if you aren't treating others differently because of the way they look, you're already on your way to becoming anti-racist. Being anti-racist begins with not being racist, but it goes beyond that. It means that you identify with *being something* rather than being *not* something.

Black people in America face racism in schools, in their communities, and in the workplace.

For example, you can be an actor or not an actor. OR, you can be an actor *or* a gamer; an actor *or* a basketball player; an actor *or* a writer; an actor *or* a scientist . . . Get the idea? If all you are is *not* an actor, you're just there, not really doing anything at all. But, if you are working at being something other than an actor, you identify with behaviors, skills, talents, and a community of people who are doing the same thing. You are actively involved, playing, writing a book, or winning a science fair; you are being something rather than *not* being something.

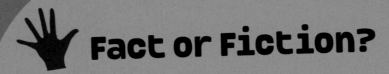

Fact or Fiction?

Anti-racists believe that no one group of people is better than another group. They also believe that our differences make each of us special. However, if you google "word origin anti-racist," one of the top results calls *anti-racist* "a code for anti-White." Some groups spread this false information to make White people afraid so they won't support anti-racism.

Being anti-racist means you are *not* being racist. But it also means you are actively helping to make sure that racism becomes less of a problem—until it hardly exists at all.

Talking to your friends about the racism they face is a good way to understand the problem—and start to work against it.

CHAPTER 2

Where Did "Race" Come From?

There are quite a few theories about where the word *race* came from. Some say it came from the French language between the 14th and 17th centuries. Others say it's an Italian or Hebrew word. But all agree that there are no races of humans. We are all categorized as *Homo sapiens*. And traits like skin, eye, and hair **pigmentation** don't change that.

Differences in skin color have **evolved** over time based on the needs of humans living in different climates. The substance responsible for skin color is called **melanin**, and it also protects the skin from sunburn and skin cancer.

Originally, people living near the equator developed more melanin and darker skin to help protect them from the sun. As people migrated farther north, many thousands of years ago, their skin began to adapt to colder climates where less protection from the sun was needed. As their need for melanin decreased, their bodies began to produce less of it. This is why the farther people live from the equator, the lighter their skin tone is.

We have all evolved with different skin tones because of the area and climate our ancestors came from, but regardless of how much melanin we have, we are all one race. How did we get to a place where we compete and struggle to get along?

Do some research online to learn how the region your ancestors are from has affected your physical characteristics.

In the 1930s, the modern idea of "race" was introduced by the National Party in Germany. The party, called the Nazis, believed there was a master race of people that was superior to everyone else. This race was made up of people descended from Scandinavian and German warriors. Anyone whose relatives weren't White with roots in Scandinavian countries or Germany was unwanted.

People who didn't belong to the "master race" were killed during the Holocaust. No one knows just how many people died, but recent estimates are as high as 15 million to 20 million. Although everyone agrees that the Holocaust was bad, there are still people who believe that one "race" is superior to another.

Why Do We All Look Different?

Scientists at the University of California, Berkeley found that human variations are a positive part of evolution. Human faces "make each of us unique and easily recognizable," and our brain is wired to be good at identifying them. Basically, human differences help you find your mom in a store or pick out your friend in a crowd.

Being Black in Nazi Germany

Hans J. Massaquoi was one of very few Black children born and raised in Nazi Germany. When he was little, he lived in a mansion with his parents and wealthy grandfather, a diplomat from Liberia. When his father and grandfather moved back to Liberia, his mother wanted to stay in Germany. They moved into a different neighborhood where no one looked like him. He was treated differently because of his color. He could not go to college, even though he was very smart. When Massaquoi was able, he left Germany for the United States. There he served in the Army, got a degree in journalism, and became a well-known author and editor. Massaquoi wrote about his life experiences in a book called *Destined to Witness*.

Nazi Germany may be the most shameful example of racism, but the Germans were not alone. Long before they promoted the idea of a superior race, people were competing and fighting with others who looked or thought differently.

A respected Greek philosopher named Aristotle (384–322 BCE) wrote that some people were born to become masters while others were born to have masters. Aristotle's writings were popular for many centuries. The Europeans and the British used Aristotle's teachings as one way to justify taking over countries when people weren't Christians. This was called colonization.

The Europeans and the British also believed in making some people from those countries work for free. This was called enslavement. They kidnapped Black people from Africa and brought them to the American colonies in the 1600s and 1700s. The Africans were not Christians and were judged to be inferior—and were sold as slaves.

Colonization had disastrous effects on indigenous populations, including war, disease, and enslavement.

In the New World, colonists encountered the indigenous people of North America. We know these diverse groups as Native Americans. They too were not Christians and were considered inferior. Colonists killed and mistreated them to get the land we now call the United States.

Like the enslaved Africans, Native Americans' skin was darker than the colonists. The colonists eventually came to the conclusion that it was not only Christianity, but whiteness that made them superior. And so the concept of "race" was born on American soil.

CHAPTER 3

Fighting Racism in the Past

Racism has a long history, but so does anti-racism. Most anti-racists fight racism because they themselves have been treated unfairly. There are also supporters who help fight racism even though they don't experience it themselves.

In America's early years, when slavery was common, some enslaved people wanted their freedom so badly that they ran away. They ran even though they knew they would be beaten or killed if they were caught. They took dangerous paths to places where slavery was illegal. The network of secret routes that people traveled to freedom was called the Underground Railroad. People who helped others gain freedom were called abolitionists. There were many well-known Black abolitionists like Harriet Tubman and Frederick Douglass. There were also many White abolitionists who helped, like Harriet Beecher Stowe and John Brown. Abolitionists were early anti-racists.

Harriet Beecher Stowe wrote *Uncle Tom's Cabin*, a book that is sometimes noted as leading to the Civil War.

Black schools did not receive the same support or funding as
White schools.

Slavery finally ended in 1865 after the Northern states won a war against the Southern states. This was called the Civil War. Sadly, people who supported slavery still believed they were superior to the people they had enslaved. Southern states created laws to keep Black people from getting an education or good jobs. Southern laws and police officers would not protect Black people. Southern hospitals would not treat them. Restaurants and hotels in the South would not serve them.

Without education, good jobs, or health care, Black people had to find ways to live a better life. They opened their own schools and colleges. They started their own banks and businesses, such as those in Harlem, New York, or on Black Wall Street in Tulsa, Oklahoma. Black people made their own movies and music. They started their own restaurants and sports leagues. They became doctors and teachers so they could take care of themselves and each other. Still, some things were harder to get, like the right to vote or own land. Black people realized that they had to pull together to stand up for their rights.

The most well-known anti-racism effort in the United States was the civil rights movement of the 1960s. These protests were well organized and had strong leaders who were able to convince all kinds of people to fight for change. The leaders were called activists.

Activists like Martin Luther King Jr., Malcolm X, and Amelia Boynton told Black people that the rights in the U.S. Constitution were meant for everyone. They convinced people to protest through rallies and marches. Sometimes the protests turned violent because protesters were hurt and angry at not being treated equally for such a long time. Sometimes protests turned violent because the police and White citizens were angry about Black people standing up for themselves. When people around the country saw protesters being attacked, some of them started showing support for Black people's struggle against racism.

Protests were only one way to fight racism. Some people became important "firsts" during this time. People like Ruby Bridges and the "Little Rock Nine" contended with threats and violence to become the first students to attend all-White schools in the South.

Others, like Barbara Jordan and Thurgood Marshall, fought racism from within the system. Barbara Jordan overcame poverty to become the first Black female congresswoman. Thurgood Marshall became the first Black U.S. Supreme Court justice.

John Lewis chose multiple paths to anti-racism. He helped Martin Luther King Jr. organize the March on Washington in 1963 and marched on "Bloody Sunday" in Selma, Alabama, in 1965. He became a six-term congressman before his death in 2020.

The civil rights movement was important because not only did Black people gain a lot of important rights, but also because laws were changed. These laws opened doors for other groups facing discrimination.

John Lewis Memorial in New York's Times Square.

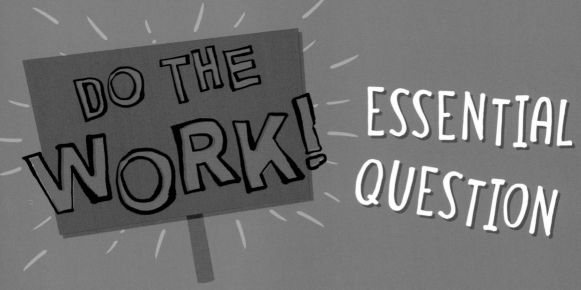

ESSENTIAL QUESTION

How can we be anti-racist?

Becoming anti-racist requires actively working against racism using words and actions. This project-based learning assignment will allow you to practice these skills. Read all the books in the *Racial Justice in America* series. Through each "DO THE WORK!" activity, you will research and put together parts of a larger project that will allow you to grow and help others grow as well.

Being anti-racist means working to eliminate racism on a daily basis. How will you work to become an anti-racist? For this portion of your project, you are going to identify things that you will do to be an anti-racist.

How will you respond when faced with injustice? What will you do with your new knowledge? How will you hold yourself and others accountable?

For the presentation of your final work, you can create a collage, magazine, podcast, jigsaw puzzle, poem, video, or social media campaign—anything to demonstrate your learning. No matter what you do, just be creative, learn something new, and publicize your work!

CHAPTER 4

Anti-Racism Today

The civil rights movement was responsible for many changes during the 1960s. Those changes did not stop racism, however. Black people and other people of color still have a harder time getting a good education. They have a harder time getting good jobs. They still have a hard time getting good health care. And they have a harder time in their encounters with police officers and the law.

There have been many legal battles and protests to help people continue to fight racism. Organizations like the National Association for the Advancement of Colored People (NAACP) and the Southern Christian Leadership Conference (SCLC) have remained strong, fighting racism behind the scenes.

Today, the Black Lives Matter movement is leading a new era in the fight for civil rights. Black Lives Matter began in 2013 as a hashtag started by three women, Alicia Garza, Patrisse Cullors, and Opal Tometi. The hashtag developed into a human rights organization that now advocates for social change.

Black Lives Matter protest, Chicago, Illinois, June 6, 2020.

In May 2020, knowledge of the Black Lives Matter movement spread worldwide. George Floyd, a Black man in Minneapolis, Minnesota, was killed by a police officer. People who witnessed the killing used their cell phones to document it. The videos shocked people and made them sad and angry. People began to realize that Black people are sometimes treated differently when they come into contact with the police. They used the hashtags #blm and #BlackLivesMatter to organize rallies to protest police violence and racism. The marches were first held in Minneapolis where Floyd died. But as the news of his murder spread, people began to protest all over the world.

Some people who joined the protests were from the Black community. They were especially sad because Floyd's murder reminded them of others who had died or were hurt because of bias and racism.

Some people who joined the protests were not from the Black community. These people are called *allies*. An ally understands that they benefit from unearned privileges based on their skin color. An ally wants to help people who do not have those privileges.

The spring and summer of 2020 saw Black Lives Matter protests all around the world.

cultural
EXCHANGE
CLUB

A school can have a population of students whose cultural backgrounds are either similar or diverse. If the cultural backgrounds at your school are similar, ask your teacher to help you find a school that has a different cultural population. Then start a cultural exchange club with them. Depending on your school's rules, you could set up class Skype or Zoom meetings. Or you could send class videos asking and answering questions about race, racism, and culture. Another idea is to have an email pen pal (talk with your teacher about school rules for pen pals). Talking about race and racism with people who might think differently than you is a good way to learn and grow as a person.

If you go to a school where students have diverse backgrounds, start a cultural exchange lunch club. One day a week, have everyone sit with someone else in the cafeteria, preferably someone from another cultural group. Make it a schoolwide activity. Not only will you get the chance to understand other cultures better, you can also make new friends.

CHAPTER 5

Doing My Part

Not everyone who wants to fight racism goes out to protest. Some people find other ways to be anti-racist. They might write articles or books. They might organize social media campaigns. Others may donate to organizations that help people affected by racism. Still others talk with friends and family about how to support people who are mistreated because of their skin color.

There is no one way to fight racism. Fighting racism can be loud, like when you chant together at a rally. It can be quiet, like when you whisper to a friend that something they said is mean or racist. Sometimes, fighting racism can be completely silent, like following a hashtag or reading a book to learn how you can get better at being anti-racist.

One way you can be anti-racist at home is to talk with your family or friends about what you're learning and how you hope to be a part of positive change. Maybe you have learned things that your parents or grandparents haven't learned. Even if they think differently about race than you do, that's okay. Maybe they will learn by watching you model being anti-racist.

At school, you can be anti-racist by standing up for people who are being treated differently because of how they look or identify. Standing up for someone can be as simple as not laughing at a racist joke or walking away from a crowd that's being mean. If you feel confident, you can even respectfully tell people engaging in racist behavior that they are being mean or hurtful.

Have you seen someone being bullied or treated unfairly because of their skin color? Talk with a parent or guardian about how you and your family can speak up when this happens. If you see something, say something.

You can be an activist at your school. You can get together with friends and form a group or club that hosts rallies or events that support anti-racism. You can start petitions with the help of a trusted adult on websites like Change.org. Or start your own podcast on Anchor.fm to talk about anti-racism and your values.

Together you can host a fund-raiser and donate to activist groups. You could even sign up with your parents and friends to march at an event in your area.

Even if no one around you thinks like you do, you can keep reading and learning. Websites like Tolerance.org and PBS.org have great anti-racist and historical articles. Smithsonian.org and YouTube have videos on many different Black history and anti-racist themes. Google searches for "Black history" and "anti-racism" will get you started. You can use your social media powers for good, sharing the content that you find.

Fannie Lou Hamer, a civil rights leader in the 1960s, said, "Nobody's free until everybody's free." Even if you aren't experiencing racism yourself, you can make the world a better place by helping others and becoming anti-racist in your own way.

Research Fannie Lou Hamer online or at your library. How could her actions inspire your anti-racism work?

EXTEND YOUR LEARNING

"European Christianity and Slavery." Lowcountry Digital History Initiative, n.d. *https://ldhi.library.cofc.edu/exhibits/show/africanpassageslowcountryadapt/introductionatlanticworld/europnea_christianity_and_slav*. Accessed August 26, 2020.

Humiliated in Hamberg. Part 4 of Exploring Human Rights in Daily Life, video series. YouTube, January 8, 2019. *https://www.youtube.com/watch?v=OtIL8_-zyNs&feature=youtu.be*.

Humphries, Monica. "Civil Rights Activists from the 1960s Share What It's Like to See Black Lives Matter Protests Spread across the Country." Insider, June 11, 2020. *https://www.insider.com/freedom-riders-civil-rights-movement-black-lives-matter-protests-2020-6*.

Massaquoi, Hans J. *Destined to Witness: Growing Up Black in Nazi Germany*. New York, NY: William Morrow and Co., 1999.

GLOSSARY

abolitionists (ab-uh-LISH-uh-nists) people who worked to put an end to slavery before the Civil War

activists (AK-tuh-vists) people who fight to bring about political or social change

advocates (AD-vuh-kates) supports an idea or a plan

bias (BYE-uhs) a personal judgment in favor of or against a thing, person, or group, usually in a way considered to be unfair

Black Wall Street (BLAK WAWL STREET) a wealthy Black community of homes and businesses in Tulsa, Oklahoma, in the early 1900s

civil rights (SIV-uhl RITES) the rights everyone should have to freedom and equal treatment under the law, regardless of who they are

discrimination (dis-krim-uh-NAY-shuhn) the unfair treatment of others based on differences in such things as age, race, or gender

evolved (ee-VOLV-d) changed gradually over a very long period of time

Harlem (HAHR-luhm) a wealthy black community and center of culture in the early 1900s

indigenous (in-DIH-juh-nuhs) having originally come from and lived in a particular region

melanin (MEL-uh-nihn) a natural brown to black coloration in skin, hair, and eyes

petitions (puh-TISH-uhnz) letters signed by many people asking those in power to change their actions or telling them how they feel about a certain issue

pigmentation (pig-muhn-TAY-shuhn) color given to a part of the body by substances in the body

racist (RAY-sist) a person who treats people unfairly or cruelly because of their race

INDEX